D0331418

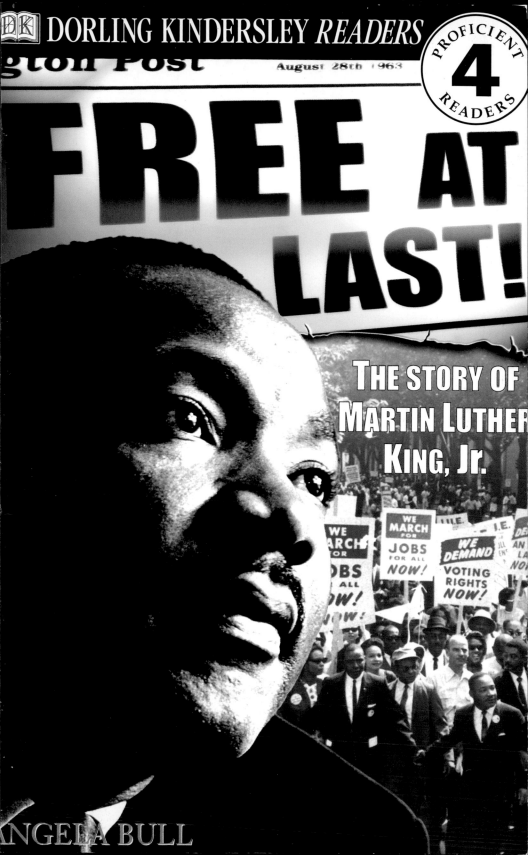

Post

August 28th 1963

FREE AT LAST!

THE STORY OF MARTIN LUTHER KING, Jr.

WE
MARCH
FOR
JOBS
FOR ALL
NOW!

WE
MARCH
FOR
JOBS
FOR
ALL
NOW!

WE
DEMAND
VOTING
RIGHTS
NOW!

I.E.
ILL
EN

I.E.
DE
LA
NO

ANGELA BULL

DK DORLING KINDERSLEY *READERS*

Level 2

Dinosaur Dinners
Fire Fighter!
Bugs! Bugs! Bugs!
Slinky, Scaly Snakes!
Animal Hospital
The Little Ballerina
Munching, Crunching, Sniffing,
  and Snooping
The Secret Life of Trees
Winking, Blinking, Wiggling,
  and Waggling

Astronaut: Living in Space
Twisters!
Holiday! Celebration Days
  around the World
The Story of Pocahontas
Horse Show
Survivors: The Night the Titanic Sank
Eruption! The Story of Volcanoes
The Story of Columbus
LEGO: Castle Under Attack!
LEGO: Rocket Rescue

Level 3

Spacebusters
Beastly Tales
Shark Attack!
Titanic
Invaders from Outer Space
Movie Magic
Plants Bite Back!
Time Traveler
Bermuda Triangle
Tiger Tales
Aladdin
Heidi
Zeppelin: The Age of the Airship
Spies
Terror on the Amazon

Disasters at Sea
The Story of Anne Frank
Abraham Lincoln: Lawyer, Leader,
  Legend
George Washington: Soldier, Hero,
  President
Extreme Sports
Spiders' Secrets
LEGO: Mission to the Arctic
NFL: Troy Aikman
NFL: Super Bowl Heroes
NFL: Peyton Manning
MLB: Home Run Heroes: Big Mac,
  Sammy and Junior
MLB: Roberto Clemente

Level 4

Days of the Knights
Volcanoes and Other Natural Disasters
Secrets of the Mummies
Pirates!
Horse Heroes
Trojan Horse
Micromonsters
Going for Gold!
Extreme Machines
Flying Ace: The Story of Amelia Earhart
Robin Hood
Black Beauty
Free at Last! The Story of
  Martin Luther King, Jr.
Joan of Arc
Spooky Spinechillers
Welcome to The Globe! The
  Story of Shakespeare's Theater
Antarctic Adventure
Space Station
Atlantis
Dinosaur Detectives

Danger on the Mountain: Scaling
  the World's Highest Peaks
Crime Busters
The Story of Muhammad Ali
LEGO: Race for Survival
NFL: NFL's Greatest Upsets
NFL: Terrell Davis
NFL: Rambling Running Backs
WCW: Going for Goldberg
WCW: Feel the Sting!
WCW: Fit for the Title
WCW: Finishing Moves
MLB: Strikeout Kings
MLB: Super Shortstops: Jeter,
  Nomar, and A-Rod
The Story of the X-Men: How it
  all Began
Creating the X-Men: How Comic
  Books Come to Life
Spider-Man's Amazing Powers
The Story of Spider-Man

A Note to Parents

Dorling Kindersley Readers is a compelling new program for beginning readers, designed in conjunction with leading literacy experts, including Dr. Linda Gambrell, President of the National Reading Conference and past board member of the International Reading Association.

Beautiful illustrations and superb full-color photographs combine with engaging, easy-to-read stories to offer a fresh approach to each subject in the series. Each *Dorling Kindersley Reader* is guaranteed to capture a child's interest while developing his or her reading skills, general knowledge, and love of reading.

The four levels of *Dorling Kindersley Readers* are aimed at different reading abilities, enabling you to choose the books that are exactly right for your child:

Level 1 for Preschool to Grade 1
Level 2 for Grades 1 to 3
Level 3 for Grades 2 and 3
Level 4 for Grades 2 to 4

The "normal" age at which a child begins to read can be anywhere from three to eight years old, so these levels are intended only as a general guideline.

No matter which level you select, you can be sure that you are helping your child learn to read, then read to learn!

LONDON, NEW YORK, MUNICH,
MELBOURNE and DELHI

Project Editor Penny Smith
Art Editors Jane Horne and
Susan Calver
Senior Editor Linda Esposito
Senior Art Editor Diane Thistlethwaite
US Editor Regina Kahney
Production Melanie Dowland
Picture Researcher Liz Moore
Jacket Designer Chris Drew
Illustrator Chris Forsey
Indexer Lynn Bresler

Reading Consultant
Linda B. Gambrell, Ph.D.

First American Edition, 2000
4 6 8 10 9 7 5 3
Published in the United States by DK Publishing, Inc.
375 Hudson Street, New York, New York 10014
A Penguin Company

Copyright © 2000 Dorling Kindersley Limited, London

Published in Great Britain by Dorling Kindersley Limited.

Library of Congress Cataloging-in-Publication Data

Bull, Angela, 1936-
Free at last! : the story of Martin Luther King, Jr. / by Angela Bull. -- 1st
American ed.
p. cm. -- (Dorling Kindersley readers)
Summary: A biography of the civil rights leader, covering his childhood,
leadership, powerful speeches, assassination, and greatest influences.
ISBN 0-7894-5716-4 (hc) -- ISBN 0-7894-5717-2 (pb)
1. King, Martin Luther, Jr., 1929-1968--Juvenile literature. 2.
Afro-Americans--Biography--Juvenile literature. 3. Civil rights workers--
United States--Biography--Juvenile literature. 4. Baptists--United States--
Clergy--Biography--Juvenile literature. 5. Afro-Americans--Civil rights--
History--20th century--Juvenile literature. [1. King, Martin Luther, Jr.,
1929-1968. 2. Civil rights workers. 3. Clergy. 4. Civil rights movements--
History. 5. Afro-Americans--Biography.] I. Title. II. Series.
E185.97.K5 B78 2000
323'.092--dc21
[B]   99-087903

Color reproduction by Colourscan, Singapore
Printed and bound in China by L. Rex

The publisher would like to thank the following for their kind permission to
reproduce their images. Key: t=top, b=bottom, l=left, r=right, c=center
Bridgeman Art Library: 7br; **Corbis UK Ltd:** 3, 6tl, 8tl, 8bl, 11tl, 13tr, 13b,
14b, 16, 17r, 20b, 21, 26r, 26-27b, 27t, 28t, 28b, 29t; **Frank Spooner Pictures:**
4tl, 6bl, 39, 47b; **Hulton Getty Images:** 4bl; **Magnum Photos Ltd:** 12, 31c,
Cartier Bresson: 18b, Cornell Capa: 47t, Bruce Davidson: 14t, 17l, 23b, 32-
33b, P. Jones: 22, Danny Lyon: 32t, W. Miller: 25b; **Popperfoto:** 10, 19, 29b,
44, 46t, 46b; **Redferns Music Picture Library:** 9br; **Science Photo Library:**
25t; **Topham Picturepoint:** 11br, 24, 30b, 40, 41t, 41b, 45.
All other images © Dorling Kindersley.
For further information see: www.dkimages.com

see our complete product line at

www.dk.com

Contents

Black in a white world   4

Bus ride to fame   12

Land of the free   18

The right to vote   30

War in Vietnam   34

The last crusade   40

Glossary   48

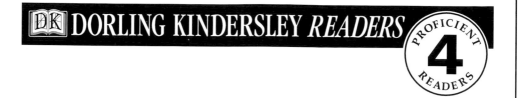
FREE AT LAST!

THE STORY OF MARTIN LUTHER KING, JR.

Written by Angela Bull

A Dorling Kindersley Book

Family home
Although his grandparents had been farm slaves, Martin grew up in a comfortable house in the state of Georgia.

Christian hero
Martin Luther was a German monk who thought people had forgotten the true teaching of Jesus. He formed a new church called the Lutherans.

Black in a white world

The small black boy looked at himself in the mirror and smiled a big smile.

"I've got a new name now!" he marveled.

Yesterday he had been plain Michael King. But today was a very special day. This morning his father, the pastor, had baptized him in church and announced his new name to the whole congregation. He was now called Martin Luther King, Jr. Junior because Martin Luther was his father's name, too. The name came from a great hero of the Christian faith.

"I'm Martin Luther King, Jr., now!" the boy thought.

His new name sounded good, and he was pleased. He grinned again. Five-year-old Martin could not guess that, one day, the whole world would know his name.

Martin was born in Atlanta, Georgia, on January 15, 1929. It was difficult being a black person in America then, especially in the southern states where Martin lived. Black people were considered inferior to whites, and laws kept them apart. They were not allowed to play in the same parks or eat in the same restaurants.

Only seventy years earlier there were slaves in the south. These were black people whose ancestors had been snatched from Africa to work on farms run by white people. Slaves had no rights. They were bought and sold like animals.

When Martin was a toddler, his best friend was a white boy. Martin was not allowed to go to the same school as his friend. Martin's father was a well-respected preacher, but Martin still had to take the worst seats on buses and at the movies.

CANADA

UNITED STATES
OF AMERICA

Chicago

Washington DC

Chester
(Crozer
College)
WEST MARYLAND
VIRGINIA
VIRGINIA

MISSOURI

KENTUCKY

TENNESSEE
Memphis Atlanta
Birmingham

NORTH CAROLINA

SOUTH CAROLINA

ARKANSAS

ALABAMA GEORGIA
Selma Montgomery

MISSISSIPPI

TEXAS

LOUISIANA

FLORIDA

MEXICO

The southern states of the U.S. are shown in dark green. Some people in the bordering states, such as Virginia, also supported slavery. This map also shows places of importance in Martin's life.

Although slavery was abolished in the southern states in 1865, the memory lingered on. Many white people still considered themselves superior. They did not want black people to swim in the same pools or sit in the same train cars.

"Whites only" signs kept black people out of many shops and even churches. This was what life was like in Martin's home town. It seemed it would be like that forever.

Freedom for all
President Abraham Lincoln signed the Emancipation Proclamation in 1863. This led to the abolition of slavery in the U.S.

Church leader
Martin's father was the pastor of the Ebenezer Baptist Church in Atlanta. More black Americans belong to the Baptist Church than any other.

Top fighter
One of the most famous black boxers of all time was heavyweight champion of the world Cassius Clay. He changed his name to Muhammad Ali.

When Martin was young, only a handful of black people had the chance to be leaders. As a church minister, Martin's father was one of the few. Martin wanted to be a leader too, but he was not sure how.

Maybe Martin could lead at school. He worked hard and usually got good marks. Or maybe he could make it to the top by fighting. He was small, but strong enough to wrestle other boys to the ground. Black men could become successful by being boxers.

Martin was also very good at speaking. He had a strong voice and a commanding way of talking. When he was 15 he entered a public speaking competition. He spoke so powerfully about "the Negro and the Constitution" that he won first prize. After the competition, Martin flung himself happily down on a seat in the bus going home.

As the bus went along, it filled up. Soon there were no spare seats. Glancing around, the white driver saw the black boy and his teacher and ordered them to stand. At first, Martin refused, but the teacher whispered a reminder of the rule, "whites before blacks." Martin got up.

"That night I was the angriest I've ever been in my life!" Martin said years later.

Second best
Black people had to stand aside for whites throughout life. Paul Robeson was a lawyer but his color lost him work. He became an actor instead.

Christianity
All Christians believe in the teachings of Jesus Christ. But there are different types of Christianity. About 25% are Protestants. The Baptists are one of many Protestant groups.

Some universities accepted black and white students.

Martin continued to wonder what career he would follow. He was athletic, clever, and a good speaker. He wanted to aim high in life. But what should he do? And in particular, what could he do to help black people?

Martin had a strong Christian faith, so he decided to follow his father and become a Baptist pastor. In 1948 he began training at Crozer College near Chester in Pennsylvania.

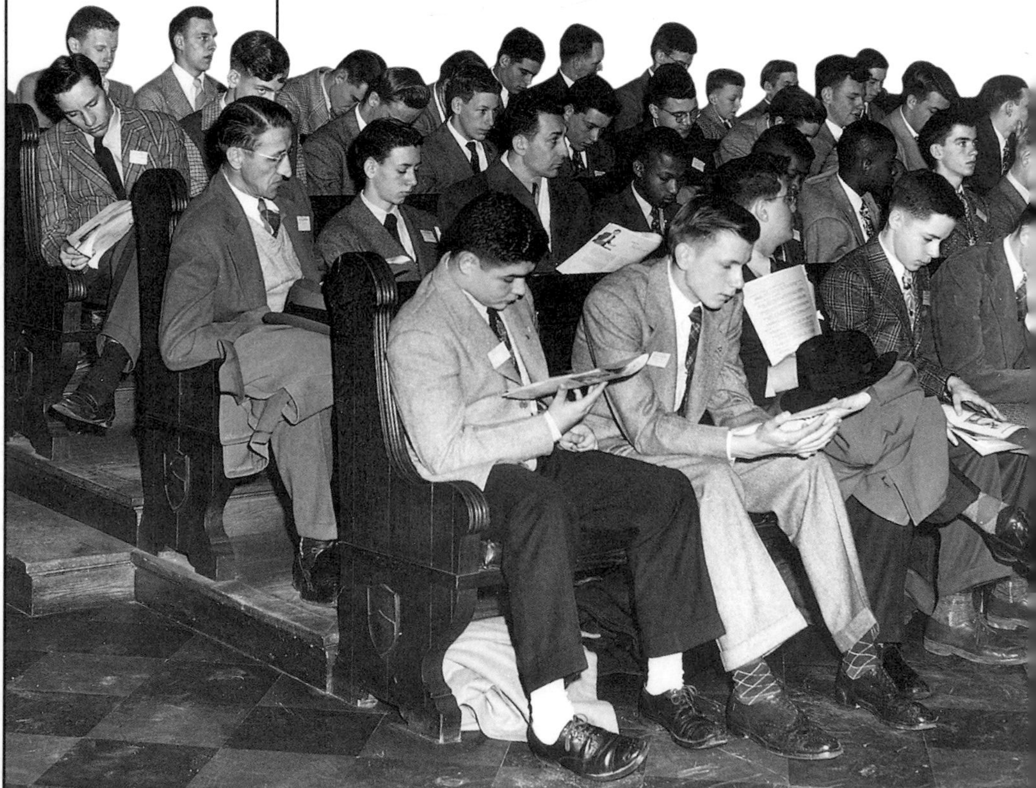

It was not always easy being a black student in a mainly white college. Martin worked extra hard to gain the respect of his fellow students. Soon he was doing well and making friends. But there was still prejudice to face, and Martin faced it with a new calmness.

Martin was studying the Indian politician Mahatma Gandhi. He was beginning to see a way to tackle the problem of discrimination – the way blacks were treated differently from whites. Gandhi had led the struggle for Indian independence from Britain by using nonviolent methods. And they had worked.

Do not fight back, Gandhi had urged. Respond peacefully to your enemies. These ideas impressed Martin. Gentleness and peace, it seemed, could overcome prejudice. Once this was defeated, other barriers would fall.

Mahatma Gandhi (Mahatma means "Great Soul")

Independent
The flag of India features a spinning wheel. This symbolizes Gandhi's great wish that the people should be self-sufficient.

Bus ride to fame

Martin finished at Crozer College at the top of his class, and by 1955 he was pastor of a church in Montgomery, Alabama. By now he had a wife, Coretta, and a baby daughter named Yolanda.

He was a happy family man. He loved preaching to his black congregation and he was good at it. His sermons were full of knowledge and passion as he described how life might be in a more equal world.

But the world was not equal and trouble was brewing. Gangs of white men had attacked black people at random all over the south that summer, and black people were growing angry. Their anger focused finally on the case of Rosa Parks.

Family life
Martin and Coretta married in 1953. After the wedding they stayed with an undertaker friend because hotels did not take black couples. They were married for 15 years and had four children.

Rosa Parks was a black seamstress. One evening after work she sank down, tired out, on a bus. Then white people got on, and the driver ordered her to give up her seat. Rosa refused. Her feet ached too much to stand. The driver called the police, and Rosa was charged with breaking the town's "whites first" bus laws.

Rosa Parks

The charge
Rosa's charge of breaking "whites first" bus laws gave black leaders a specific case to fight. "Disorderly conduct" was the usual charge when black people stayed seated.

On the buses
Before the boycott, 70% of bus passengers were black, but there were no black bus drivers.

Men at the top
The Civil Rights Movement had other leaders who worked alongside Martin. These included the Reverend Ralph Abernathy, Martin's chief supporter and friend.

The story of Rosa Parks reminded Martin of how a bus driver had forced him to stand the night he won his speaking prize. Burning with anger and sympathy, he called a meeting at his church.

A huge crowd turned out. Resentment was growing over the treatment of black people and they were demanding action. Already some black people were collecting weapons to fight against whites.

Martin spoke powerfully. People must reject violence, he said. Instead, they should boycott the bus company – simply refuse to use the buses. If the bus company lost money, it would rethink its "whites first" attitude.

Martin and others distributed thousands of leaflets urging the boycott. They organized a pool of cars with black drivers to provide rides for black passengers.

On the first day of the boycott Martin went nervously out into the street. He saw a few cars, then a bus roared along. It was empty; so was the next – and the next. He watched the buses all morning. Hardly any black passengers rode on them.

The boycott was working well. But true success would only come when the first passengers on a bus, black or white, could keep their seats.

At church Martin said they should continue the boycott. "If we protest courageously, with dignity and Christian love, we shall win," he said.

Car ownership
In the 1800s a person carrying a red flag had to walk in front of a car. This warned of an unsafe vehicle on the road. But speed and safety improved and by 1955 three quarters of American families owned their own cars.

Hatemail
People who send hate mail sometimes cut out letters from newspapers and stick them down so they cannot be identified as the sender.

Under arrest
Martin was arrested a total of 16 times for his protests.

Days passed and the boycott held strong. But Martin began to get hate mail from angry whites. Some letters contained death threats.

Then one evening when Martin was out, Coretta went to get baby Yolanda, who had been sleeping at the back of the house. At that moment there was a loud boom! The house filled with smoke as a bomb exploded at the front. It was a miracle no one was hurt.

Two months after the boycott began the city authorities discovered an obscure law that banned boycotts. Martin was arrested and fined.

But black people were not willing to give in, so the boycott continued.

Then the car-pooling system was declared illegal. The police arrested Martin again for helping to organize it. As Martin's trial began, a reporter rushed in with dramatic news. The Supreme Court had declared that the bus segregation that kept black and white people apart went against the Constitution of the United States. This meant that black and white people now had equal rights on the local buses. The boycott was no longer necessary and Martin's trial was stopped. His peaceful campaign had succeeded.

Next day, in a mood of celebration, Marin and his friends boarded their first integrated bus!

Supreme Court
This is the highest court in the United States. It has a chief justice and eight associate judges. They make the final decision on certain law cases.

Fair ways
The U.S. Constitution was drawn up in 1787 and went into effect in 1789. The Constitution set out ideas for a fair and free country outside British rule.

Book writer
Stride Towards Freedom: The Montgomery Story was Martin's first book. He wrote five others.

Speech writer
Martin worked hard on his speeches – in 1957 and 1958 he made 208 of them.

Land of the free

Black people could now keep their seats on Montgomery buses. But other laws stopped them from being treated the same as white people. Martin wanted all America to hear his side of the story so he wrote a book called *Stride Towards Freedom: the Montgomery Story.*

He told of the bus boycott and pleaded for equal rights.

The book sold well. Martin spoke about it on TV and autographed copies in bookstores. But some – even a few black people – did not want change. As he signed books in New York, a black woman approached.

"Are you Martin Luther King?" she asked.

Martin said that he was. Suddenly the woman raised her fist. There was a letter knife in it! She plunged it down into Martin's chest.

Martin stayed calm as he was rushed to the hospital. The knife was so close to the main artery of his heart that any sudden movement, even a sneeze, could have killed him.

As he recovered, a white girl sent him a letter. "I'm writing to say I'm so happy you didn't sneeze," she said.

Home viewing
TV was first demonstrated in 1926 by John Logie Baird. By the 1950s most families had a black and white set. Television helped to spread news about the Civil Rights Movement.

Attacker
Isola Curry, the woman who stabbed Martin, was found to be insane. She was sent to a hospital for criminally insane people.

Places to eat
Sit-ins occurred in places such as Woolworth's five-and-tens and local restaurants that served lunch to workers. Fast food was just being introduced in the U.S.

After Martin recovered from the attack, he decided to give up his church ministry and move back to Atlanta. Here he devoted his time to campaigning for equal rights.

Lunch counters with "whites only" notices were the first target. Groups of black people were already "sitting in" at these counters, waiting peacefully to be served, and refusing to leave.

Many students took part in the sit-ins. They followed nonviolent rules, were polite, and did not strike back if they were abused.

At these demonstrations the students sang the hymn of the movement: "We shall overcome! We shall overcome one day!"

As the sit-ins began to work, Martin's followers tried a new kind of protest. They wanted black people to have equal rights on buses that traveled across states. So they organized the Freedom Rides.

Black and sympathetic white people ignored "whites only" signs as they traveled from state to state. In some places buses were burned and Freedom Riders were beaten.

Eventually the Supreme Court said that segregation on buses was illegal. The Civil Rights Movement had won another battle!

Famous song
Laws against black people were called Jim Crow laws after an old minstrel song.

No ride
Martin was on probation when the Freedom Rides took place and would not risk a jail sentence by joining them. This caused resentment among some of the riders.

Martin's campaign moved to Birmingham, Alabama. This was the most segregated city in the United States, with "whites only" restaurants, libraries, and parks. Even a storybook about a white rabbit marrying a black rabbit was banned!

As black people protested, white groups reacted violently. They beat and stabbed black protesters and blew up a black church.

By now black children wanted to help. Martin agreed to let them join the marches. So children and students filled the street and moved peacefully forward.

"Stop!" the police ordered.

But the marchers continued.

Then firemen unwound their powerful hoses and pointed them at the children. Water blasted out, soaking the young protesters and knocking them to the ground.

Then snapping, snarling police dogs were released on the wet and frightened children.

The children's ill treatment made many adults join in demonstrations. Eventually the Alabama Supreme Court made a ruling. The city must remove its "whites only" signs.

"Birmingham will never be the same again," Martin declared.

Dog's life
Police dogs are used in crowd control and to sniff out drugs. Most police dogs are German shepherds, which are clever and easy to train.

Protesters being hosed in Birmingham, Alabama, in 1963.

U.S. Congress
The people who make laws and fix taxes are members of Congress. This has two separate houses. The upper house is the Senate, with two senators from each state. The lower is the House of Representatives.

Martin's message was being noticed across America, and in the highest places too.

On June 11, 1963, President John F. Kennedy made a speech on national television. The president called for equality. He wanted all American citizens to be treated the same, no matter what their color.

Soon afterward President Kennedy submitted a Civil Rights Bill to Congress. The bill outlawed every kind of segregation and promised funding to enforce the law.

Lower House
The House of Representatives has 435 members from across the U.S. The number from each state depends on the population in that state.

Martin was delighted. This was just what he wanted. A great wave of support grew for Martin's non-violent ideals. "Whites only" notices were torn down in dozens of hotels and schools across the country.

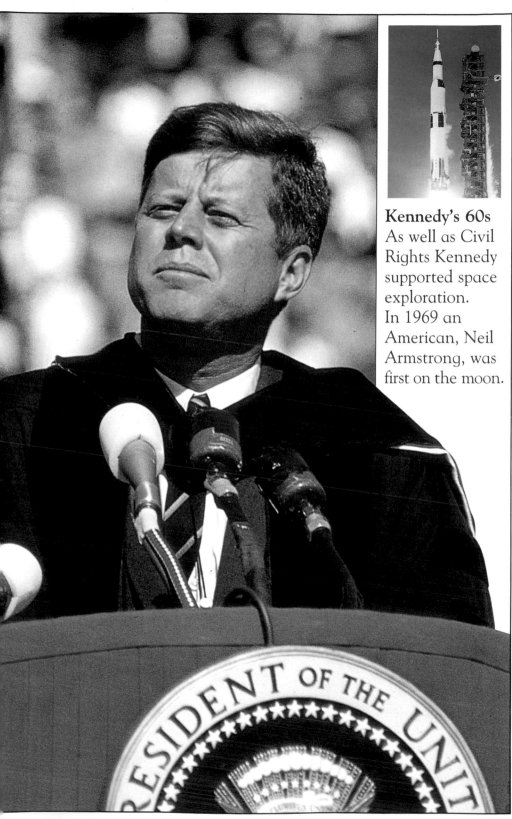

Kennedy's 60s
As well as Civil Rights Kennedy supported space exploration. In 1969 an American, Neil Armstrong, was first on the moon.

The Lincoln Memorial in Washington, D.C.

War leader
Abraham Lincoln was president during the Civil War fought between Union states in the north and Confederate slave states in the south. In 1865 Lincoln led a Union victory.

A hundred years had passed since slavery was abolished. Martin wanted to mark this. So he called for people to gather in Washington, D.C.

On August 28, 1963, a quarter of a million marchers gathered by the Lincoln Memorial. They burst into loud applause when Martin stood up to speak. It was the biggest occasion in Martin's life and he rose to it.

"Now is the time to lift our nation from the quicksands of racial injustice to the solid rock of brotherhood!" he boomed.

The cheers rose louder as Martin described his vision of the future.

"I have a dream today!" he thundered. He told them that he dreamed that the sons of slaves and the sons of slave owners would one day sit together as brothers.

He called for the day when all God's children would join hands and sing, "Free at last, free at last. Thank God Almighty, we are free at last!"

The applause was tremendous.

U.S. capital Washington, D.C., was named after the first president of the United States, George Washington. The grand city design is based on Paris.

President John Kennedy was riding through Dallas, Texas, when he was shot in the head. The killer was thought to be Lee Harvey Oswald.

Taking over
Lyndon B. Johnson was Kennedy's vice-president. When Kennedy died Johnson was sworn in as president.

For a brief time Martin's vision of freedom and equality swept America. Black people could go to more of the places that used to be reserved for whites. Martin was named *Time Magazine*'s Man of 1963.

But the good times did not last. On November 22, 1963, Martin was watching television when a news announcer interrupted with dramatic news. President Kennedy had been shot and killed.

People across America mourned the president. And with his death, the Civil Rights Movement suffered a serious setback. Many white people liked the old ways. Although President Johnson, Kennedy's successor, signed the Civil Rights Bill, the bill did not tackle all the problems black people faced.

Martin receives the Nobel Peace Prize

Then the following October, Martin received the immense honor of the Nobel Peace Prize. This prize is given to people who had worked hard in the cause of peace. Martin was only 35 years old, the youngest person ever to win the prize.

As the chairman of the Norwegian Parliament presented it, he called Martin "the first person in the western world to show that a struggle can be waged without violence."

War and peace
Alfred Nobel invented dynamite. Money from this invention is given every year in Nobel prizes.

The Nobel Peace Prize medal

29

Right to vote
In Selma there were 15,000 black people but only 150 were registered to vote.

The right to vote

By Christmas 1964, Martin had chosen a new goal – to uphold the right of black people to vote. The Civil Rights Bill guaranteed this right, but many southern towns refused to register black voters.

One such town was Selma, Alabama. The town was in old slave territory and its sheriff believed in keeping black people down.

Martin Luther King (far right) talks to Selma's sheriff (far left).

Selma's sheriff was not alone in thinking Martin a troublemaker. Some members of Washington's central government felt the same way, and the FBI had already begun to monitor his phone calls.

When Martin visited Selma and spoke there, the Alabama state police looked on and took notes. Martin promised the disgruntled black community a mass march from Selma to Montgomery, the state capital, to demand voting rights.

Planning the march was difficult. And matters became even worse when black people began to join a new militant movement called Black Power.

Since Martin had so many opponents, the sheriff felt safe in banning the march. But Martin would not be stopped. As he led a line of marchers through Selma, he was arrested and jailed again.

Law enforcers
The Federal Bureau of Investigation, or FBI for short, has files of over 250 million sets of fingerprints.

Black Power
Originally called Malcolm Little, Malcolm X was a Black Power leader. He thought black people should live in their own communities without white interference.

Go to jail
Prisoners were often crammed into dirty cells infested with cockroaches. At night they slept on filthy mattresses. The food could be as little as two cups of black-eyed peas and two slices of bread a day.

Martin's arrest made the headlines. From prison, he sent a letter to the *New York Times*. "There are more negroes in jail with me," he wrote, "than there are on the voting rolls."

Released on bail, Martin planned a new march from Selma to Montgomery. This time state police attacked the marchers with whips and batons wrapped in barbed wire. Tragically, they shot a young man to death.

Still Martin would not give up. Suddenly he received unexpected help from President Johnson, who had been shocked by news stories of the violence. He announced new laws to enforce the right to vote.

When an Alabama judge approved a new march, a crowd of black marchers triumphantly crossed the state. Martin's feet hurt, but he did not mind. "We are on the move," he declared, "and no wave of racism can stop us."

Bad news
Newspapers and TV showed the world what was happening to Martin Luther King's peaceful movement. Ill treatment of black people by white police encouraged broad-minded white people to join the Civil Rights Movement.

War in Vietnam

By 1966 Martin had shown how effective determination and peace could be. Nonviolence had succeeded in Montgomery, Birmingham, and Selma. Now he decided to head north to Chicago, where many black people lived in slums. He planned to campaign for decent houses and peaceful streets.

Chicago is the birthplace of the skyscraper.

But there was a new and complicating situation – the Vietnam War, which had begun in 1965. American soldiers were fighting against communism in a country far from home, and Martin did not like it.

He was publicly opposed to violence and had even won the Nobel Peace Prize for his non-violent views. He hated war, and did not hesitate to let President Johnson know his feelings. A gap opened between the two men, who had been so close on civil rights.

When Martin wanted President Johnson's support for his Chicago campaign the president refused it. Martin had criticized the government and spoken out in public against the Vietnam War. Many called him a communist.

Vietnam War (1965–75) America supported South Vietnam against the communist Vietcong who ruled the north.

Communism Communists believe people should share all things equally. In communist countries the communist party has total control.

Communist symbol

Taking a stand
The Black Power salute was first seen at the 1968 Mexico Olympics. When medals were presented to winning black athletes they raised clenched fists in gestures of defiance.

Door fame
Martin's action mirrored that of his namesake's, Martin Luther, who nailed a protest to a church door.

Martin also faced another problem. To his dismay, the Black Power Movement was growing. Many young black people thought that peaceful means had not achieved enough. They wanted direct, violent action – like the war they were watching on TV every night. When Martin spoke at a meeting, explaining his ideas, Black Power members booed him.

Despite his problems, Martin moved into a slum area of Chicago and went ahead with his campaign. He asked for better housing for black people and an end to police brutality and mass unemployment.

When he stuck his demands on the door of City Hall, Chicago's Mayor Daley was scornful. He said that these demands were unnecessary. Chicago already had a massive social program.

This northern city was not responding as the southern cities had done. Martin felt out of touch with its politics and its people. He saw black people rioting against the police, and he was horrified by their guns and the hatred in their faces. During one march, a brick was thrown at him. Baffled and depressed, Martin finally left Chicago.

Northern life
Although black people could mix freely with white people, they still had a lower standard of living.

Gun point
The U.S. Constitution says all citizens have the right to carry arms to defend themselves.

Martin leads a march in Chicago, August 1966

Martin was exhausted by years of campaigning. He needed a vacation. He chose a house on Jamaica, where there was no telephone and nobody to interrupt him.

As he sat gazing over the sea, Martin thought about the Civil Rights Movement and achievements of individual black people. He thought about Black Power. And he thought about the Vietnam War. He decided to write a book to clarify his ideas. It was called *Where Do We Go from Here?*

Martin was still thinking about the Vietnam War when he returned from Jamaica. The huge sums spent on the war gobbled up the money that black people needed. He wanted an anti-war rally to take place in New York. But the government brushed Martin's views aside. Martin started to be known as "Martin Loser King."

Vacation spot
Jamaica is a large island in the Caribbean. Its beautiful mountains, forests, and sandy beaches make it a popular vacation destination.

Bad language
In *Where Do We Go from Here?* Martin talked about how the word "black" also meant dirty or bad, while "white" meant clean or good. He said that language had to change to stop black children from feeling bad about themselves.

Poverty trap
Martin felt that being poor took away people's right to "the pursuit of happiness" because poor education, bad housing, and limited job opportunities kept them trapped in poverty.

The last crusade

Angered by the failure of his anti-war rally, Martin began to plan something even bigger and bolder. He had come to realize that black people were not the only ones suffering. He dreamed of bringing together representatives of America's 35 million poor people – black, white, and Indian – to Washington, D.C., for a tent-in.

Many white people in the U.S. are poor.

Ideal home
The White House is the home of the U.S. President. It takes its name from its white-painted walls. Besides offices and rooms for the president's family to live in, it contains a movie theater, gym, swimming pool, and solarium.

They would camp peacefully opposite the White House until the government promised them the fair treatment they deserved.

Martin's friends opposed this extravagant crusade. But the more they tried to stop Martin, the more determined he grew. There must be a total reconstruction of society for the benefit of everyone, he argued, and the whole system of government must be disrupted to bring this about.

Camping out
A year after Martin planned his great "tent-in," 400,000 people gathered at Woodstock for the world's biggest outdoor music festival. Its theme was love and peace.

41

Memphis
Standing on the Mississippi River, Memphis is named after an ancient Egyptian city on the Nile River.

Memphis man
Elvis Presley made his first recording in Memphis.

Meanwhile, back south in Memphis, Tennessee, trouble was brewing. Some black sanitation workers had gone on strike. They wanted to earn the same money as white people doing the same job.

Although Martin was busy with his Washington campaign, he accepted an invitation to lead a peaceful protest march. He flew into Memphis on March 28, 1968.

Nobody told him that there was a Black Power base in Memphis. He only realized this when the march deteriorated into savage fighting. Black Power marchers swung clubs, police fired, protesters were injured, and one boy was killed.

Martin was devastated. When he later watched television clips of the march, they showed black teenagers starting the violence. Martin knew then that the whole concept of nonviolent protest was on trial, and himself with it.

He left Memphis, promising to be back in a week to lead a massive, nonviolent rally.

Lorraine Motel
Martin stayed at the Lorraine Motel for black people. He had a room on the second floor, overlooking the carpark and swimming pool. The motel is now a Martin Luther King museum.

James Earl Ray
Ray belonged to a political party that hated black people. One party member had offered a reward of $30,000 to anyone who killed Martin.

Martin was as good as his word. He returned to Memphis on April 3 and checked into a motel.

Yet something was making him nervous. Suddenly he did not want to address a rally that evening. Only his friends' pleas changed his mind.

So he addressed the crowd. He reminded them of how close to death he had sometimes been. But his own life did not matter, he said. God had shown him the Promised Land – freedom and justice lay ahead for black people.

The cheers were as enthusiastic as Martin could have wished. Encouraged, he returned to his motel.

But there was another newcomer in Memphis that night – an escaped convict named James Earl Ray. He had studied newspapers that criticized Martin for stirring up violence. Ray hated black people. And he had a gun.

45

Simulated telescopic gunsight showing scene of Martin's assassination

Life for killer
James Earl Ray fled to England but was brought back to the U.S. to stand trial. He pleaded guilty and was sentenced to 99 years in prison. He was still in custody when in died in 1998 aged 70.

Martin spent April 4, 1968, quietly in his Memphis motel, making plans for the forthcoming march. In the evening he dressed to go out to dinner with friends.

James Earl Ray had booked into a rooming house and requested a room at the back. It overlooked the Lorraine Motel where Martin was staying. Ray had a pair of binoculars and a high-powered rifle.

At about six o'clock Martin stepped out onto his balcony. Friends were joking in the parking lot below. Martin called down to them, leaning on the balcony rail. Suddenly a gun blazed. Martin crashed to the floor.

"Oh, my God! Martin's been shot!" a friend screamed.

People rushed forward to give first aid and call an ambulance. But it was no use. Martin died as soon as he reached the hospital.

The whole world was shocked. Many people wanted to say how much they had admired this passionate, peaceful campaigner.

Thousands of people attended his funeral in Atlanta, with millions more watching on television. At the funeral people sang the words Martin had quoted in his great "dream speech": "Free at last, free at last. Thank God Almighty, we are free at last!"

In memory
The third Monday in January is now a national holiday in Martin's memory. His birthplace and grave are both national historic sites.

REV MARTIN LUTHER KING, JR.
1929—1968

Free at last, Free at last
Thank God Almighty
I'm free at last

Glossary

Assassination
The murder of a well-known person.

Baptize
To name someone in a religious ceremony. The person is sprinkled or dipped in water.

Black Power
An organization that tries to gain influence for black people.

Boycott
An organized action in which people refuse to use or buy something until their demands are met.

Car pools
Groups of people who "pool" together and travel in one car.

Civil Rights
The rights to equal opportunities in all things including jobs, education, and housing.

Communism
A way of life in which there is no private property. Everything is owned by everyone.

Congregation
People who gather together to attend a church service.

Congress
The national governing body of the United States. Men and women are elected to Congress.

Constitution
The written set of rules that describes how the government works and the rights of individual people in the U.S.

Discrimination
When people are treated unfairly because of their race, religion, or gender.

FBI
Federal Bureau of Investigation, a U.S. law-enforcement organization.

Freedom Riders
Black and white people who traveled across the United States on buses to protest segregation.

Hate mail
Letters and parcels sent to threaten or frighten the receiver.

Integrate
When different races mix together freely.

Jim Crow
Racial discrimination against black people. It is named after a minstrel song.

Ku Klux Klan
An organization of white people who believe the white race is better than all others. The Ku Klux Klan tries to prevent black people from having any power.

Minister
Someone who works for the church. A minister gives help and advice and performs religious ceremonies.

Prejudice
An unreasonable low opinion of something or someone.

Racism
Disliking someone because of his or her race or color.

Rally
A mass meeting of people for a common cause.

Segregation
Separating groups of people such as black and white people.

Sit-ins
The occupation of all or part of a building by people protesting about an injustice.

Slavery
When men and women are owned by other people. Slaves have no rights to anything.

Social program
A plan to improve the living and working conditions of disadvantaged people.

Supreme Court
The highest court in the U.S. It makes the final judgment on certain law cases.

Index

Abernathy, Reverend Ralph 14
Alabama Supreme Court 23
arrests 16, 31, 32
Atlanta, Georgia 6, 47

baptism 4
Birmingham, Alabama 22
Black Power 31, 36, 42
salute 36
bomb 16
boxers, black 8
boycott of bus company 14–17
bus segregation 17, 21
buses
across states 21
Atlanta 9
Montgomery 13, 14

car-pooling 14, 17
Chicago, Illinois 34
children, ill treatment 22–23
Christianity 10
Civil Rights Bill 24, 28, 30
Civil Rights Movement 14, 28, 33
Clay, Cassius 8
communism 35
Congress 24
Constitution 17, 37
Crozer College 10, 12
Curry, Isola 19

Daley, Mayor 36
death 46
death threats 16

Emancipation Proclamation 7

fast food 20
FBI 31

fire hoses 22
Freedom Rides 21
funeral 47

Gandhi, Mahatma 11
guns, right to have 37

hate mail 16
home, family 4

"I have a dream" 27

Jamaica 39
Jim Crow laws 21
Johnson, Lyndon B. 28, 33, 35

Kennedy, John F. 24, 28
King, Coretta Scott 12
King, Martin Luther, Sr. 4, 6, 8
King, Michael 4
knife attack 19
Ku Klux Klan 22

laws against black people 6, 18
Lincoln, Abraham 7, 26
Lincoln Memorial 26
Lorraine Motel 44, 46
lunch counters 20
Luther, Martin 4, 36

Malcolm X 31
marches 22, 26, 31
marriage 12
Memphis, Tennessee 42, 44
Montgomery, Alabama 12
Muhammad Ali 8

national holiday 47
Nobel Peace Prize 29
nonviolence 11, 14

Parks, Rosa 12, 13

police dogs 23
poor people/poverty 40
prisoners 32

rally, Memphis 44
Ray, James Earl 44, 46
riots, black 37
Robeson, Paul 9

Scott, Coretta 12
segregation, outlawing of 24
Selma, Alabama 30
sit-ins 20
slave ships 6
slaves 4, 6, 7
slums, Chicago 36
speaking, public 8
speeches 18, 26
state police 31, 32
Stride Towards Freedom 18
student demonstrations 20, 21
Supreme Court 17, 21

tent-in, Washington, D.C. 40
TV news 19

Vietnam War 35
violence 42
vote, black right to 30, 33

Washington, D.C. 26, 27, 41
Washington, George 27
"We shall overcome!" 21
Where Do We Go from Here? 39
white gangs 12, 22
White House 41
whites before blacks 9, 13
whites only 7, 20, 22
Woodstock festival 41

PROFICIENT 4 READERS

Martin Luther King Jr. had a dream that one day all people would be treated as equals, whatever the color of their skin.

BEFORE WE'LL BE A SLAVE, WE'LL BE BURIED IN OUR GRAVE

BEFORE WE'LL BE A SLAVE, WE'LL BE BURIED IN OUR GRAVE

DORLING KINDERSLEY *READERS*

Stunning photographs combine with lively illustrations and engaging, age-appropriate stories in DORLING KINDERSLEY *READERS*, a multilevel reading program guaranteed to capture children's interest while developing their reading skills and general knowledge.

1 BEGINNING TO READ	Beginning to read	• Word repetition, limited vocabulary and simple sentences • Picture dictionary boxes
2 BEGINNING TO READ ALONE	Beginning to read alone	• Longer sentences and increased vocabulary • Information boxes full of extra fun facts • Simple index
3 READING ALONE	Reading alone	• More complex sentence structure • Information boxes and alphabetical glossary • Comprehensive index
4 PROFICIENT READERS	Proficient readers	• Rich vocabulary and challenging sentence structure • Additional information and alphabetical glossary • Comprehensive index

With Dorling Kindersley Readers, children will learn to read – then read to learn!

Dorling DK Kindersley

ISBN 0-7894-5717-2   Printed in China

$3.99 USA
$5.95 Canada

see our complete product line at
www.dk.com

9 780789 457172   90000